# Traditional
# Slow Airs
# of Ireland

## Tomás Ó Canainn

More than 100 of the most
beautiful Irish Airs.
Suitable for all instruments.

ISBN 978-0-946005-84-0

Visit Hal Leonard Online at
**www.halleonard.com**

Contact us:
**Hal Leonard**
7777 West Bluemound Road
Milwaukee, WI 53213
Email: info@halleonard.com

In Europe, contact:
**Hal Leonard Europe Limited**
42 Wigmore Street
Marylebone, London, W1U 2RN
Email: info@halleonardeurope.com

In Australia, contact:
**Hal Leonard Australia Pty. Ltd.**
4 Lentara Court
Cheltenham, Victoria, 3192 Australia
Email: info@halleonard.com.au

Music Typesetting by Tomás Ó Canainn.
Continuity & layout by Grace O'Halloran, Mary Madigan and Charlie Nicholl.
Design by John Loesberg.
Cover Picture by Richard Haughton.
Special thanks to all the artists who appear on the companion recording.

Audio containing every single air from this book is available too:

**Traditional Slow Airs of Ireland**
**HL14033982**
**Ossian OSSCD 118/119**
Edited and produced by Tomás Ó Canainn

Slow Airs played by:
**Pat Aherne** (guitar) , **Ray Barron** (bouzouki) ,
**Tomás Ó Canainn** (uilleann pipes, accordion) ,
**Tony Caniffe** (mandolin) , **Johnny McCarthy** (whistle, flute, fiddle) ,
**Aisling Casey** (oboe) , **John O'Connor** (soprano saxophone) ,
**Bríd Cranitch** (piano) , **Matt Cranitch** (fiddle) , **Séamus Creagh** (fiddle) ,
**Con Ó Drisceoil** (accordion) , **Bonnie Shaljean** (harp) ,
**Niall Vallely** (concertina), **Tony O'Flaherty** (Low Whistle)
Songs sung by:
**Dónal Mac a'Bháird** (Caitlin Triall) ,
**Sinéad Cahir** ( The Month of January) ,
**Tomás Ó Canainn** ( Iníon an Fhaoit) ,
**Seosamh Ó h-Éanai** (Caoineadh na dTrí Muire)

# Introduction

The slow air is rightly regarded as one of the most beautiful facets of the Irish musical tradition and yet many of the better dance-music executants never attempt the playing of an air. I hope that the hundred slow airs notated here and played on the accompanying recordings will inspire such performers to enter the magical world of the air. A well-played air has a splendid, soaring dimension that must be experienced to be understood. Perhaps some words of explanation may help towards that understanding.

Many of the airs have come to us as the music of sean-nós (old style) songs or even as ballads. An acquaintance with the singing tradition is clearly a help, though not a necessity, in the playing of an air. For that reason, I have included songs on the demonstration recordings, so that the change from song-air to slow-air might be more easily understood. There are four good songs here which have their corresponding slow airs in this collection.

Some of the airs notated here are by Carolan, while others are unconnected with songs, as far as we know, but have become established as purely instrumental pieces. "Lament for Staker Wallace" and "O'Donnell's Lament" are but two examples of such well-known airs.

Generally speaking, if a tune has been around for a considerable time and has been transmitted orally, I would call it traditional, whatever its original source. The word *tradition* implies many things which I shall not discuss here: for a more detailed analysis I would refer the interested reader to my other book *Traditional Music in Ireland*, also published by Ossian.

## ORNAMENTATION

As in all unaccompanied musical traditions, some form of ornamentation is involved in the playing of Irish slow airs. The performer must be guided by his or her instinct for the tradition. My own advice is to err on the side of too little ornamentation rather than overburdening the air with the kind of decorative excesses that were not uncommon in some eighteenth and nineteenth century collections of Irish music.

I would regard ornamentation as a way of easing movement between the main notes of a melody — a kind of musical lubrication which makes the progression logical and inevitable. The listener must not have his or her attention drawn specifically to the ornamentation by the performance, as that, in itself, would be a sure sign of excessive decoration.

## PHRASING

Ornamentation normally occurs within the framework of a musical phrase, which is the basic building-block of the air. In each of the airs in this book, phrases are indicated by slurs around the series of notes. I think one might regard the actual phrasing as a movement from the first note of the phrase to the final, which I regard as a resting place — a plateau where one may pause to look around for the next resting point, which is, of course, the final note of the next phrase.

The best advice I can give – and I think it will improve your slow-air playing enormously – is to make a definite pause on the last note of the phrase, holding it for about twice its indicated length. This, more than any other recommendation of mine, will make the airs notated in this book spring to life. You should feel that each phrase is an inevitable progression to that vitally important final note. Movement to the next phrase is reminiscent of a singer taking a breath before singing out the next series of notes. Such an approach to phrasing implies that the time-signatures quoted for these airs is merely an approximation. You should never feel that you are playing out a series of notes in regular 3/4 or 4/4 time: what you produce must be an attractively fluid outpouring of music, dominated by its phrasing.

I have pointed out above that many of the airs are derived from songs and that a knowledge of traditional singing would be of some help in decorating an air, but I should point out that instrumental ornamentation is not at all the same as vocal ornamentation. The best guide to instrumental decoration of an air is the instrument itself: I feel strongly that slow-air players should, to a large extent, submit their playing to the conventions of their particular instrument and the way it is played traditionally.

This means, of course, that a fiddler and a piper will adopt different approaches to playing an air and their performances will, in general, be quite different from what an accordionist, a tin-whistler, a flute-player or a concertina player will produce. I cannot sufficiently emphasise that you should be guided by the instrument and by your own traditional experience. If that experience is limited, I suggest you listen a lot to the accompanying tape before you attempt to play. You will here various instruments playing the airs on the cassette tapes. If you have not previously heard airs played on bouzouki, oboe or saxophone, my best advice is to listen with an open mind. You may be surprised!

## VARIATION

As your air-playing improves, you will realise that there are no unbreakable rules involved. Experience will teach you that the phrasing recommended here, for example, is not the only phrasing possible. This should lead you to experimenting with slightly different phrasing every time you play a tune. Equally, your overall performance will improve if you employ somewhat different ornamentation for each appearance of a particular phrase. But only do this if you are confident in your ability to make the new variation sound just right and completely unforced.

## VIBRATO

A small, regular variation in the pitch of anote, i.e. vibrato, is sometimes used by fiddlers and pipers in the playing of slow airs. There are two schools of thoughts on the whole question of the use of vibrato in the playing of Irish traditional slow-airs: some feel that it is out of place and changes the character of the music, while others accept it without question. Whichever camp you follow, I think you should eschew the wide vibrato that orchestral string players use, as it is not suitable for the playing of airs. A more restrained and narrower vibrato, not unlike the natural vibrato of the human voice is what is needed. I feel that it should be restricted to the longer, more important notes of the melody. One sometimes hears accordionists and concertina players attempting vibrato by a kind of continuous bellows-quivering. In the hands of a sensitive performer it can sound effective, though it is clearly related to changes in the volume of a note, rather than in its pitch. Some fiddlers vary the finger-pressure on the string, with no visible lateral movement, while others make a quite definite lateral movement, with a corresponding wide pitch variation: there is no hard-and-fast rule, but good-taste and a feeling for the tradition should be your guide.

## ACKNOWLEDGEMENT

*I learned much about the playing of airs from my former colleagues in the traditional music group, NA FILÍ. It is a pleasure to acknowledge here the debt I owe to Réamonn Ó Sé, Tom Barry and Matt Cranitch, whose air-playing was always inspirational.*

Tomás Ó Canainn.

Airs carried on air:
Melody that fingers
Unfold, decorate.
Breathing bellows an elbow
Continues to pump: swelling
Lung that forces a chanter
To speak.

(From 'Melos" by Tomás Ó Canainn)

# Contents

## 1. Siubhán Ní Dhuibhir

## 2. Fáth Mo Bhuartha

11

## 3. Cití na gCumann

## 4. Cath Chéim an Fhia

## 5. Táimse ar an mBaile Seo

## 6. Lament for Staker Wallace

## 7. Geaftaí Bhaile Buí

## 8. Cailín na Gruaige Doinne

## 9. Conlach Ghlas an Fhómhair

## 10. Caoineadh na dTrí Muire

## 11. An Caisideach Bán

17

## 12. Amhrán na Trá Báine

## 13. Maidin Luan Cincíse

## 14. Príosún Chluain Meala

19

## 15. Tabhair Dom Do Lámh

20

## 16. An Droighneán Donn

♩ = 60

## 17. Planxty Irwin

♩ = 80

## 19. Caoineadh Uí Dhónail

## 20. Caiseal Mumhan

## 21. Eleanor Plunkett

## 22. Bánchnoic Éireann Ó

## 23. Caitlín Triall

♩ = 60

## 25. Munster Cloak

## 26. Carrickfergus

## 27. Is Trua gan Peata an Mhaoir Agam

## 28. Dónal Óg

## 29. Sliabh na mBan

♩ = 60

## 30. Fáinne Geal an Lae

## 31. Cuan Bhéil Inse (Amhrán na Leabhar)

31

## 32. Conneries

## 33. Princess Royal

## 34. Buachaill ó'n Éirne

## 35. The Banks of the Suir

## 36. Iníon an Fhaoit

## 37. Eibhlín a Rúin

## 38. Snowy−Breasted Pearl

## 39. Eochaill

## 40. Anach Cuan

## 41. The Trip We Took Over the Mountain

## 42. An Brianach Óg

## 43. Do You Remember That Night?

## 44. Lord Inchiquin

## 45. Róisín Dubh

## 46. Sliabh Geal gCua

## 47. The Wounded Hussar

43

## 48. An Sceilpín Droighneach

## 49. Airde Cuan

44

## 50. Contae Mhuigheo (Paddy Lynch's Boat)

## 51. Wild Geese

## 52. Seán Ó Duibhir

♩ = 50

## 53. Baptist Johnston

♩ = 70

48

## 55. An Raibh Tú ar an gCarraig?

## 56. Blind Mary

50

## 58. An Buachaillín Bán

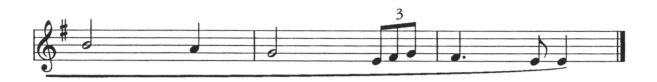

## 59. Spailpín a Rúin

♩= 70

## 60. Aisling Gheal

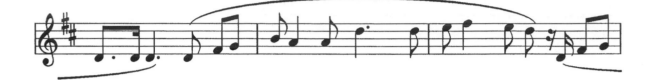

## 61. Port Gordon

## 62. Cois a' Ghaorthaidh

## 63. Fanny Power

## 64. A Stóir Mo Chroí

## 65. Speic Seoigheach

## 66. Caoineadh an Spailpín

## 67. Cape Clear

## 68. Port na bPúcaí

## 69. Lament for the Fox

## 70. Úna Bhán

## 71. Máirin de Barra

## 72. An Londubh is an Chéirseach

## 73. Death and the Sinner

## 74. General Monroe's Lament

## 75. Mo Mhúirnín Bán

## 76. An Ciarraíoch Mallaithe

♩ = 40

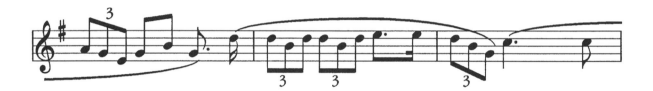

67

## 77. Loch na gCaor

♩ = 60

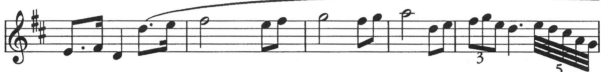

## 78. Éamonn Mhagáine

## 79. Páistín Fionn

## 80. Fox's Sleep

## 81. Cuaichín Gleann Neifín ('Glenroe' Theme)

71

## 82. Tiarna Mhuigheo

## 83. George Brabazon

## 84. Glenswilly

## 85. Siúl a Ghrá

## 86. Buachaill Caol Dubh

## 87. Jimmy Mo Mhíle Stór

## 88. Lagan Love

## 89. Beinsín Luachra

## 90. Cill Chais

77

## 91. Banks of Sullane

## 92. Éamonn a' Chnuic

## 93. Down by the Sally Gardens

## 94. An Spailpín Fánach

## 95. Drimín Donn Dílis

## 96. Bean Dubh a' Ghleanna

## 98. Gile Mear

## 99. Bunclody

## 100. An Leanbh Sí

## 101. Planxty Hewlett

## 102. Slán le Máigh (The Bells of Shandon)

## 103. The Coolin

## 104. Bunnán Buí

## 105. Easter Snow

## 106. Cáit Ní Dhuibhir

## 107. Maighdean Mhara

## 108. An Goirtín Eornan

## 109. Morgan Magan

♩= 60

## 110. The Month of January

## 111. Bridín Bhéasach

## 112. Marbhna Luimní

## 113. Úir Chill a' Chreagáin

### 114. De Bharr na gCnoc

## 115. Ráiteachas na Tairngreacht

## 117. O'Rahilly's Grave

## 118. Rosc Catha na Mumhan

# Alphabetical Index